MACMILL
INTERME

JOHN STEINBECK

The Pearl

Retold by M.J. Paine

MACMILLAN

MACMILLAN READERS

INTERMEDIATE LEVEL

Founding Editor: John Milne

The Macmillan Readers provide a choice of enjoyable reading materials for learners of English. The series is published at six levels – Starter, Beginner, Elementary, Pre-intermediate, Intermediate and Upper.

Level Control
Information, structure and vocabulary are controlled to suit the students' ability at each level.

The number of words at each level:

Starter	about 300 basic words
Beginner	about 600 basic words
Elementary	about 1100 basic words
Pre-intermediate	about 1400 basic words
Intermediate	about 1600 basic words
Upper	about 2200 basic words

Vocabulary
Some difficult words and phrases in this book are important for understanding the story. Some of these words are explained in the story, some are shown in the pictures, and others are marked with a number like this: ...[3]. Words with a number are explained in the Glossary at the end of the book.

Answer Keys
Answer Keys for the *Points for Understanding* and *Exercises* sections can be found at www.macmillanenglish.com

Contents

	The People in This Story	4
	Introductory Note	6
1	Kino, Juana and Coyotito	7
2	The Doctor	13
3	Kino Finds a Pearl	17
4	Kino's Dream	24
5	The Doctor Comes	30
6	Kino Tries to Sell the Pearl	40
7	The Trouble Begins	49
8	Fire and Death	54
9	Kino and Juana Run Away	61
10	The Trackers	68
11	The Cry of Death	76
12	Kino and Juana Return Home	83
	Points for Understanding	86
	Glossary	89
	Exercises	91

The People in This Story

Kino

Juana

Coyotito

Apolonia

Doctor

Pearl Buyer

Juan Tomas

Trackers

Introductory Note

This is a story about Kino, his wife Juana and their baby Coyotito. Kino was a poor Mexican-Indian. He made his money by fishing for pearls – valuable stones found inside the shell of oysters. Kino's life was poor and simple until he found the largest pearl in the world. He thought that the pearl would bring happiness to his family. But instead of happiness, the pearl brought fear and danger.

1
Kino, Juana and Coyotito

Kino woke up early in the morning. The stars were still shining in the sky. The cockerels were beginning to crow[1] and the pigs were looking for something to eat. Outside the little wooden house, some birds were singing and moving in the bushes.

Kino opened his eyes and looked at the light coming in the door. Then he looked at the box where his son, Coyotito, was sleeping. The box hung on ropes from the roof. Lastly, Kino turned his head towards Juana, his wife. Juana lay beside him on the mat. Her shawl covered her body and half her face. Juana's eyes were open. Her eyes were always open when Kino woke up. Juana had eyes like little stars. She was looking at Kino as he woke up.

Kino could hear the sound of the waves on the beach[2]. The sound of the waves was like music in the early morning. Kino's blanket covered his nose because the air was cold. He turned his head and saw Juana. She was quietly getting up. She went to the hanging box where Coyotito slept. She bent over and comforted Coyotito. The baby looked up for a moment, then closed his eyes and slept again.

Juana went to the little fire. She took a piece of coal and blew it until it started to burn. Then Juana put pieces of wood on the fire. Kino got up and pulled his blanket around his head and shoulders. He pushed his feet into his sandals and went outside. He stood and watched the sun come up.

Kino sat down outside the door and pulled the blanket round

Kino's blanket covered his nose because the air was cold.

his knees. He looked at the little red clouds high over the sea. A goat came near and looked at Kino. Behind Kino, the fire began to burn brightly. Kino could see the flames and the light through the door. He could see the flames through the holes in the walls of his little house, too. Juana was busy making corncakes[3] for breakfast.

Suddenly, the sun came up out of the sea. The sun was so bright that Kino covered his eyes. He could see Juana making the corncakes. Kino could smell the corncakes cooking, too. A thin, frightened dog came up and lay down next to Kino. The morning was beautiful, like every other morning.

Kino heard Juana take Coyotito out of his hanging box. Juana washed the baby and pulled her shawl round him. She held Coyotito close and fed him. Kino could hear these things without looking at them. Juana was singing an old song. She sang the song in many different ways. The song comforted Kino. The song comforted Coyotito, too.

Kino, Juana and Coyotito

There was a wooden fence around Kino's house. On the other side of the fence, there were some more houses. Smoke came from these houses and Kino could hear people having breakfast. But these sounds were not like the sounds in Kino's house. His neighbours'[4] wives were not like Juana, either.

The morning air was not so cold now and Kino pulled the blanket from his face. Kino was young and strong. His black hair hung down over his brown forehead. He had hard, bright eyes and a thin, strong moustache.

Yellow sunlight fell on the house. Near the wooden fence, two cockerels started to fight. Kino watched the cockerels for a moment. Then Kino watched some birds flying towards the hills. The world was awake now. Kino got up and went into his little wooden house.

Juana was sitting near the fire. She got up as Kino came through the door. Juana put Coyotito back into his hanging box. Then she combed her black hair and tied it back with thin, green ribbon.

Kino sat by the fire and ate a hot corncake. He only had corncakes and milk for breakfast. When Kino had finished eating, Juana came back to the fire. She ate her breakfast, too. Kino and Juana were both happy. There was no need to talk.

The sun was warming the little house. The light shone through the holes in the walls. The light shone on Coyotito. Coyotito was in his hanging box. Something moved on one of the ropes. Kino and Juana stood quite still and looked. A scorpion was coming slowly down the rope and its tail was straight out behind. A scorpion's tail has a sting in the end, a sting that kills. The tail can bend over the scorpion's head, when it wants to sting somebody.

Kino was breathing loudly through his nose, so he opened

his mouth to stop the noise. The scorpion moved slowly down the rope, towards the box. Juana prayed silently. Kino moved very quietly across the room, with his hands in front of him. His eyes were on the scorpion. Under the scorpion, in the hanging box, Coyotito laughed and put up his hand. The scorpion saw the hand and stopped. The scorpion's tail bent over its head. Kino could see the sting in the end of its tail.

Kino stood very still and moved his hand forward very slowly. The scorpion's tail bent over again. At that moment, Coyotito touched the rope and the scorpion fell. Kino put his hand forward very quickly, but the scorpion fell past Kino's fingers, onto the baby's shoulder. The scorpion stung Coyotito.

Kino cried out like an animal. He took the scorpion and pressed it between his hands. Kino threw the scorpion down and beat it into the ground. Coyotito screamed with pain in his box.

Juana took the baby in her arms. She found the red wound[5]. She put her lips over the wound and sucked. Juana sucked hard and spat out the poison. She sucked again and Coyotito screamed. Kino stood and watched. He could do nothing.

The neighbours heard the baby's screams and they came out of their houses. Kino's brother, Juan Tomas, stood in the door with his fat wife, Apolonia, and their four children. All the neighbours tried to look into the room. One small boy was trying to see between the neighbours' legs. The people in front spoke to the people behind.

'A scorpion!' they said. 'A scorpion has stung the baby!'

Juana stopped sucking the wound for a moment. The wound was red and getting bigger. All of these people knew about scorpions. A man can be very ill from the poison, but a baby can easily die. First, the wound gets bigger, then the baby is hot and has a pain in the stomach. A baby can easily die if enough poison goes into the wound.

The pain of the sting was going away. Coyotito stopped screaming and began to cry quietly. Juana was a little woman, but she was very strong. She always did what Kino wanted and she was always happy. She could work hard and go without food, almost better than Kino could. When Juana was ill, she didn't need a doctor. But now Juana did a very surprising thing.

'The doctor,' she said. 'Go and bring the doctor.'

2
The Doctor

'The doctor will not come,' the people in the doorway said.

'No,' Kino said to Juana. 'The doctor will not come to us.'

Juana looked at Kino. Juana's eyes were cold. Coyotito was Juana's first baby. He was the most important thing in Juana's life.

'Then we will go to the doctor,' Juana said.

Juana put one end of her shawl over her head. She put the other end of the shawl over the baby's eyes. The people in the doorway pushed against the people behind and Juana went out of the house. Kino and Juana went out of the gate to the little path and the neighbours followed. They were all going to the doctor with Kino and Juana.

They all walked quickly to the centre of the town. Juana and Kino were first. All the neighbours and their children were following. The sun made black shadows on the ground. All the people and the black shadows moved quickly towards the town.

They came to a place where the little wooden houses ended and the stone houses began. The city had houses with big walls and cool gardens. Red and white flowers hung over the walls. Juana and Kino could hear little birds in cages singing in the gardens.

The poor people crossed the square and passed in front of the church. More people were following Kino and Juana now. Everyone was talking about Coyotito and the scorpion. The

The Doctor

people knew that Kino and Juana were taking their baby to the doctor.

The beggars[6] in front of the church looked at Kino and Juana. The beggars looked at Juana's old, blue skirt and the holes in her shawl. They looked at Kino's old blanket. They could see that Kino was poor. The beggars followed, because they wanted to see what was going to happen.

The beggars knew everything in the town. They knew about the little crimes and the big crimes. The beggars slept outside the church. No one could enter without the beggars knowing.

The Doctor

And the beggars knew the doctor, too. They knew that the doctor was no good. They knew that he loved money more than anything else. They also knew that the doctor could not make people better. They had seen the dead bodies go into the church.

There was nobody in the church now. There was nobody in the church with money, so the beggars followed Kino and Juana. They wanted to see what the fat, lazy doctor was going to do for a poor baby with a scorpion's sting.

The crowd of people came to the big gate in the wall of the doctor's house. They could smell the food cooking in the doctor's house. Kino stopped and thought about the doctor.

The doctor was not of the same race[7] as Kino. The doctor's race had beaten and robbed Kino's race for nearly four hundred years. Kino always felt afraid and angry when he came near people of the doctor's race. Kino felt that he could kill the doctor more easily than he could talk to him. People of the doctor's race spoke to all of Kino's race as if they were animals.

Kino raised his right hand to knock at the door. He felt angry. His lips were tight against his teeth, but he took off his hat with his left hand. Kino knocked at the gate and waited. Coyotito cried a little in Juana's arms. She spoke quietly to the baby. The crowd pushed nearer to see and hear.

After a moment, the big gate opened a few inches. The man who opened the door was a man of Kino's race. Kino spoke to him in their Indian language.

'My little boy,' Kino said. 'A scorpion has stung my little boy.'

The door started to close. The servant refused to speak in the Indian language.

'Wait a moment,' the servant said in Spanish, and shut

The Doctor

the door. The bright sun threw the people's shadows on the white wall.

The doctor sat on the bed in his room. He was wearing a dressing-gown made of red silk. The dressing-gown came from Paris. He was drinking hot chocolate from an expensive cup. The doctor held the cup gently between his fingers. The doctor was fat and he did not look happy.

There was a little bell and some cigarettes on a table beside the doctor. The furniture and curtains in the room were heavy and dark. The pictures in the room were religious and there was a large, coloured photograph of the doctor's wife. She was dead.

The doctor drank a second cup of chocolate and ate a biscuit. The servant from the gate came to the open door and waited.

'Yes?' the doctor asked.

'A little Indian with a baby is here,' the servant replied. 'A scorpion has stung his baby.'

The doctor put his cup down slowly, then he got angry.

'Have I nothing better to do than make little Indians well?' he shouted. 'I am not an animal doctor!'

Then the doctor thought for a moment and spoke again.

'Indians never have any money,' said the doctor. 'Go and see if the Indian has any money.'

'Yes, sir,' said the servant.

The servant opened the gate a little and looked at the waiting people. This time, the servant spoke in the Indian language.

'Have you any money?' he asked.

Kino put his hand under his blanket. He brought out a piece of paper. He slowly opened the paper so that the servant could see eight pearls. The pearls were ugly and grey and almost without value. The servant took the pearls and closed the gate again. This time, he soon came back. He opened the gate and gave the pearls to Kino.

'The doctor has gone out,' he said. 'He was called to a man who is very sick.'

Then the servant shut the gate quickly because he felt ashamed[8].

Now, all the people felt ashamed because they could not help Kino. They slowly went away. The beggars went back to the church steps. Kino's friends went home. They tried to forget Kino and Juana and the shame that they felt.

Kino and Juana stood in front of the gate for a long time. Kino slowly put his hat on his head. Then, suddenly, Kino hit the gate with his hand. He looked down, surprised at the blood running between his fingers.

3
Kino Finds a Pearl

The little wooden houses of the fishing people were built near the beach, on the right of the town. There were canoes in front of the houses. Kino and Juana came slowly down the beach to Kino's canoe. Kino's canoe was the most valuable thing he owned. The canoe was very old. It had belonged to Kino's father and grandfather in the old days. Now it belonged to Kino.

Kino finds a Pearl

A canoe was valuable because a man could get food with it. If a man had a canoe, he could always give a woman something to eat. If a man had a canoe he did not need to fear hunger. Every year, Kino covered his canoe with plaster[9] which his father had taught him to make. The plaster hardened on the outside of the canoe and made it strong and safe.

Now Kino came to the canoe. He laid his diving stone, his basket and ropes in the bottom of the canoe. Then he folded his blanket and laid it in the boat.

Juana laid Coyotito on the blanket. She put her shawl over him, so that the hot sun could not shine on him. Coyotito was quiet now. But the wound made by the scorpion's sting was getting worse. Juana could see that the poison had gone up to his neck and under his ear. Coyotito's face was red and hot.

Juana collected some brown seaweed[10] and put it on the baby's shoulder. Seaweed was as good a medicine as the doctor could have given to Coyotito. But because this medicine was simple and didn't cost anything, people didn't think it was much good.

Kino finds a Pearl

The dangerous stomach pains had not come to Coyotito. Perhaps Juana had sucked out the poison in time, but she still worried about her first-born child. Juana had not prayed directly to God for Coyotito to get better. Instead, she had prayed that Kino might find a pearl. Then they would have money to pay the doctor.

Kino and Juana pushed the canoe down the beach, into the water. Juana climbed in and Kino pushed the back of the boat. Kino walked in the water beside the canoe until it floated on the little waves. Then Kino and Juana paddled the canoe forward. It moved quickly through the water. The other pearl fishermen had gone out to sea before Kino and Juana. In a few moments, Kino could see the fishermen in their boats above the oyster beds[11].

The oyster beds were very valuable because any oyster might have a pearl in it. Pearls are made by accident. A small piece of sand hurts the flesh of the oyster. The oyster then covers the piece of sand with smooth plaster. This plaster becomes hard like rock and turns into a pearl. If the oyster covers it again and again, the pearl becomes bigger and more valuable.

In the past, these oyster beds had made the King of Spain very rich. And because he was rich, he had become very powerful. The pearls from these oyster beds had helped the King of Spain to pay for his wars. Men have dived for oysters for centuries. They collect the oysters from the bottom of the sea and open them to look for pearls.

Kino had two ropes. One was tied to a heavy stone and the other was tied to a basket. Kino took off his shirt and trousers and put his hat in the bottom of the canoe. The water was as smooth as oil. Kino took his stone in one hand and his basket

Kino finds a Pearl

in the other. He put his feet over the side of the canoe and the stone pulled him down to the bottom of the sea. Bubbles came up behind Kino until the water cleared and he could see clearly. He looked up. The surface of the water was like a bright mirror and he could see the bottom of the canoe.

Kino moved carefully so that he did not fill the water with mud and sand. He put his foot on his stone. He worked quickly as he pulled the oysters away from the bottom of the sea.

Kino's people sang songs about everything that had ever existed or happened. They sang songs about the fishes, about the angry sea and about the calm sea. They sang songs about the light and the darkness, and about the sun and the moon. Everyone knew these songs. As Kino filled his basket, he could hear the songs of the sea in his head. Kino was holding his breath and he could also hear his heart beating.

Kino finds a Pearl

Little fish swam by and Kino thought of another song. This song was 'The Song of the Pearl that Might Be', because every shell he threw into his basket might contain a pearl. It was not easy to find a pearl, but Kino might find one with luck and the help of God. Kino knew that Juana was praying in the canoe above him. Juana was praying very hard for Kino to be lucky. She wanted a large pearl because it would buy medicine for Coyotito.

Kino was young and strong. He was very proud that he could stay under the water for more than two minutes and collect the largest shells. The oyster shells were shut tight because Kino was moving them. A little to Kino's right, there was a rocky little hill covered with young oysters that were not yet ready to be collected. Then, just near a little rock, Kino saw a very large oyster lying by itself.

The shell was partly open. Inside, Kino saw something shining, and then the shell shut quickly. Kino felt excited. He pulled the oyster loose and held it tightly. He kicked his foot free from the stone. His body rose to the surface and his black hair shone in the sunlight. Kino put his

Kino finds a Pearl

arm over the side of the canoe and laid the oyster in the bottom.

Juana held the boat still as Kino climbed in. Kino's eyes were shining with excitement as he slowly pulled up his stone. Then he pulled up his basket of oysters and lifted it in. Juana could see that Kino was excited. She pretended not to look at the large oyster. Juana always thought that if she wanted something too much, the luck might go away. Juana stopped breathing as Kino slowly opened his short, strong knife. He looked thoughtfully at the basket. Perhaps he should open the big oyster last. Kino took a small oyster from the basket, cut the flesh and searched inside. Then he threw the oyster back into the sea.

Then Kino looked at the big oyster. He sat in the bottom of the canoe, picked up the shell and looked at it for a long time. The oyster was shining black and brown. Now Kino felt that he did not want to open the oyster. The shine that he had seen inside might only be a little piece of shell. Under the water, a man could see many things that were not real.

Juana's eyes were looking at Kino and she could not wait. She put her hand on top of Coyotito's covered head.

'Open it,' she said softly.

Kino quickly pushed his knife into the shell. The shell tried to close, but Kino pushed hard and the shell fell open. The flesh of the oyster moved, then was still. Kino lifted the flesh and there lay a great pearl. The sunlight fell on the pearl and made it shine like silver. It was the largest pearl in the world.

Kino finds a Pearl

Juana held her breath and made a little noise. 'The Song of the Pearl' was loud in Kino's head. This shiny pearl would make all of Kino's dreams come true. Kino picked the pearl out of the oyster and held it in his open hand. He turned the pearl over and saw that it was very beautiful. Juana looked at the pearl in Kino's hand. That hand had hit the doctor's gate. The broken flesh had turned grey and white in the sea water.

Without thinking, Juana went to Coyotito, who was lying on his father's blanket. Juana lifted the seaweed and looked at Coyotito's shoulder.

'Kino,' she cried suddenly.

Kino looked up and saw that the poison was going out of the baby's shoulder. He saw that the poison was going out of Coyotito's body. Then Kino's hand closed over the pearl and he put back his head and cried out loudly. His eyes rolled and his body was stiff as he screamed towards the sky. The men in the other canoes looked up, surprised. Then they paddled quickly towards Kino's canoe.

4
Kino's Dream

People do not know how news travels through a town, but it travels very fast. News travels faster than small boys can run. It travels faster than women can talk about their neighbours.

Kino and Juana and the other fishermen came to Kino's little wooden house. The town was already full of the news that Kino had found the biggest pearl in the world. Mothers had heard the news before their little boys could tell them.

The news reached the little wooden houses and spread among the stone houses where the rich people lived. When the priest heard the news, he thought of the repairs[12] that his church needed. The priest thought about the value of the pearl. He tried to remember if Kino had ever brought Coyotito to the church. The priest tried to remember if he had married Kino and Juana. The news came to the shopkeepers and they looked at the things that they had not sold.

The news reached the doctor, too. He was sitting with a very old woman. The woman's only sickness was old age, but the doctor would not tell her because he wanted her money. When the doctor heard about Kino's pearl, he thought for a long time.

'I am looking after his son,' the doctor said. 'I am giving the child medicine for a scorpion bite.'

The news about the pearl came to the beggars in front of the church. The beggars laughed with pleasure. They knew that a

Kino's Dream

poor man who suddenly becomes rich always gives money to beggars.

The men who bought the pearls from fishermen were called buyers. These buyers sat in their little offices in the town. When a fisherman brought in some pearls, the buyers argued and shouted until the fisherman took a very low price. When the buyers had bought some pearls, they sat alone. Their fingers touched the pearls and played with them. But the buyers did not really own the pearls. There was only one rich buyer and he paid the other buyers to work for him.

The news about Kino's pearl came to these men. Their eyes became thoughtful and they dreamt of owning this large pearl. Each man thought that the rich buyer would not live forever. When the rich buyer died, someone had to take his place. Each man thought that if he had enough money, he could become a rich buyer, too.

Many people were interested in Kino now. Something strange happened to each person when they heard about Kino's pearl. The pearl became a part of everyone's dreams.

It became part of their hopes and part of their plans[13] for the future. The pearl became part of everyone's wishes and needs.

Only one man stopped these people from having the pearl. That man was Kino. And so Kino became everyone's enemy.

The news of the pearl brought something black and bad to the town. This black and bad thing was like a scorpion. The town seemed to have become full of poison.

Kino and Juana did not know these things, because they were both so happy and excited. Kino and Juana thought that everyone was happy and excited. In the afternoon, when the sun had gone over the mountain into the sea, Kino sat in his little wooden house. Juana sat beside him. The house was full

Kino's Dream

of neighbours. Kino held the great pearl in his hand and the pearl felt warm and alive. The neighbours looked at the pearl in Kino's hand. They asked themselves how such luck could come to any man. Kino's brother, Juan Tomas, sat beside Kino.

'What will you do, now that you have become a rich man?' he asked Kino.

Kino looked at his pearl. Juana looked down and covered her face with her shawl so that the neighbours could not see her. Kino looked into the shining pearl and dreamt of all the things that he had always wanted to do. In the pearl, Kino saw Juana, Coyotito and himself in the church. Kino and Juana were being married because now they could pay the priest.

'We will be married – in the church,' said Kino softly.

In the pearl, Kino saw how they were dressed. He dreamt of their wedding. Juana was wearing a new shawl and a new skirt. Under the long skirt, Kino could see that Juana was wearing shoes. Kino himself was dressed in new, white clothes and he carried a new hat. Coyotito also wore shoes. He wore a blue sailor suit from the United States and a little cap. Kino saw all of these things in the shining pearl.

'We will have new clothes,' he said.

Then Kino dreamt of more things that he could buy with the pearl. Now that he was rich, he could buy a rifle. Kino saw himself in the pearl, holding a rifle. Everything that Kino saw was a dream, but it was a very pleasant dream.

'A rifle. Perhaps,' said Kino softly. 'I will buy a rifle.'

The neighbours, who were listening in silence to Kino, nodded their heads. A man sitting at the back said softly, 'A rifle. Kino will have a rifle.'

Juana looked at Kino. Her eyes opened wide at the things Kino had said. A new strength seemed to have come to him.

Kino's Dream

Kino looked again into the pearl, and had another dream. He saw Coyotito sitting at a little desk in a school. Kino had once seen a desk through an open door. Coyotito was dressed in a jacket and he had a white collar and a wide, silk tie. And Coyotito was writing on a big piece of paper. Kino looked at his neighbours.

'My son will go to school,' he said, and the neighbours were silent.

Juana looked up in surprise. Her eyes were bright as she looked at Kino. Then she looked down quickly at Coyotito in her arms.

Could all this be true? she thought.

'My son will open books and read,' Kino continued. 'My son will learn to write and know about writing. Coyotito will learn numbers, too. These things will make us all free, because if Coyotito knows, then we will all know.'

Kino looked into the pearl again. He saw himself and Juana sitting by the fire in the little wooden house, while Coyotito was reading from a big book.

'The pearl will do all these things,' Kino said.

Kino had never spoken so many words in his life and suddenly, he was afraid of his talking. Kino's hand covered the pearl because he was so afraid.

The neighbours knew that they had seen something great. They knew that they would talk about Kino and the pearl for many years. If Kino's dreams came true, the neighbours would be able to say how Kino's eyes had shone. The neighbours would say that some great power had entered Kino and that he had become a great man.

If Kino's dreams did not come true, the neighbours would say something different. They would say that a foolish madness

Kino's Dream

had entered Kino and that he had spoken many foolish words.

Kino looked down at his closed hand. The skin was white where he had hit the doctor's gate.

The evening was coming and it was getting dark. Juana carried the baby in her shawl. She went and put some small pieces of wood on the fire. The fire burnt up and the flames shone on the neighbours' faces. The neighbours knew that it was time to go home. But they did not want to leave. They stayed in the house until it was almost dark and Juana's fire was making big shadows on the walls. Then they suddenly started to whisper to one another.

'The Father is coming. The priest is here.'

The men took off their hats and stepped back from the door. The women covered their faces with their shawls and looked down. Kino and his brother, Juan Tomas, stood up. The priest came in. He was an old man with grey hair and sharp eyes. He thought that the people were like children and he spoke to them like children.

'Kino,' he said softly. 'You are named after a great man, who was a great father of the Church.'

The priest made his words sound very important.

'The man that you are named after taught the people many important things. Didn't you know that?' asked the priest. 'It is written in books.'

Kino looked quickly down at Coyotito's head. Kino thought that one day his son would know the things that were written in books. Kino did not feel so happy now. He looked at his neighbours to see what could have made him feel so different. The priest spoke again.

'I hear that you have found a great pearl.'

Kino opened his hand and held it out. The priest

breathed quickly as he saw the size and beauty of the pearl.

'I hope that you remember to give thanks to God, who gave you this pearl,' the priest said. 'I hope that you will pray to God to help you in the future.'

Kino nodded his head without speaking, but Juana answered softly.

'We will, Father, and we will be married now. Kino has said so.'

Juana looked at her neighbours and they all nodded their heads.

'It is nice to see that your first thoughts were good thoughts,' the priest said. 'God bless you, my children.'

The priest turned and left quietly, and the people moved back to let him pass. But Kino's hand closed tightly on the pearl and he looked around. He was beginning to be afraid again.

The neighbours went home and Juana sat by the fire. She put the pot of boiled beans over the little flame. Kino walked to the door and looked out. He could smell the smoke from all his neighbours' fires. Kino could also see the stars in the sky. He began to feel cold, so he covered his nose with his blanket.

The thin dog came to him and shook itself. Kino looked down, but he did not really see the dog. He felt alone in the world and he did not feel safe. The night insects[14] seemed to be singing about something bad. Kino shook a little and pulled his blanket more tightly against his nose. He still held the pearl and it felt warm and smooth in his hand.

Kino could hear Juana behind him. She was making cakes near the little fire. For a few moments Kino felt safe. Then, he felt afraid again. Kino was afraid of making plans. He knew that it was dangerous to make plans. Bad things happen to a man who makes too many plans.

Kino wanted the money that the pearl would bring him. He wanted to send Coyotito to school. He had so many plans. But it was dangerous to make plans and Kino was afraid of the danger. But he wanted the money. Kino stood at the door and looked out into the night.

5

The Doctor Comes

While Kino was standing at the door, he saw two men coming. One of the men was carrying a light, which shone on the ground and on the man's legs. The men came through the opening of Kino's wooden fence and then came to the door. Kino saw that one of the men was the doctor and the other was the doctor's servant.

'I wasn't at home when you came this morning,' the doctor said. 'When I heard about your baby, I came as quickly as I could.'

Kino stood in the door, with hate[15] burning in his eyes. He was afraid again. He was afraid because the doctor's race had beaten and robbed Kino's race for hundreds of years.

'The baby is nearly well,' Kino said quickly.

The doctor smiled, but his eyes did not smile.

'Sometimes, my friend,' the doctor said, 'a baby that has

The Doctor Comes

been stung by a scorpion will begin to get better, then suddenly…'

The doctor made a little noise with his lips, to show how quickly death could come.

'Sometimes,' the doctor said again, 'a sting will leave a thin leg, or a blind eye, or a bent back. Oh, I know about scorpion stings, my friend. I can make your baby better.'

Kino felt even more afraid. He did not know about scorpion stings. The doctor had read many books. Perhaps the doctor was right. Kino was angry at himself and at the doctor. He was angry at himself because he had not learnt to read books. He was angry at the doctor because the doctor knew this.

Kino did not know what to do. He felt sure that the doctor was telling lies. But he could not do anything which might be bad for his son, Coyotito. He stood back and let the doctor and the servant enter the little house.

Juana stood up from the fire as the doctor came in. Juana covered the baby's face with her shawl. When the doctor went to her and held out his hands, Juana held the baby close to herself. She looked at Kino. The shadows from the fire were moving on his face. Kino nodded and Juana let the doctor take Coyotito.

'Hold the light,' the doctor said. The servant held the light high and the doctor looked at the wound in the baby's shoulder. The doctor thought for a moment, then he pulled back the baby's eyelid and looked at Coyotito's eyes. The doctor nodded his head as the baby moved about in his arms.

'I thought this would happen,' the doctor said. 'The poison has gone in and the baby will soon get worse. Come, look!'

The doctor looked into the baby's eye. Kino looked and saw that the eye was a little blue. Kino did not know whether the

The Doctor Comes

eye was always blue or not. He did not know whether to believe the doctor or not. But there was nothing Kino could do.

The doctor took a little bottle of pills from his bag. Then he took Coyotito and pressed the baby's lips until Coyotito opened his mouth. The doctor's fat fingers put the pill far back on the baby's tongue, so that Coyotito could not spit the pill out. Then the doctor took a jug of water and gave Coyotito a drink. The doctor looked again at the baby's eyes and then gave Coyotito back to Juana.

'I think that the poison will get worse in about an hour,' the doctor said. 'The medicine may save the baby. I will come back in an hour. Perhaps I am in time to save your son.'

The doctor took a deep breath and went out of the house. The servant followed with the light.

Juana held Coyotito under her shawl. She looked at the baby and she was worried and frightened. Kino came to her. He lifted the shawl and looked at his son. Kino moved his hand to look under the eyelid. Then he saw that the pearl was still in his hand. He went to a box by the wall, took a piece of cloth from the box and put the pearl in it. Then Kino went to a corner of the little house and made a little hole in the floor with his fingers. He put the pearl in the hole and covered it with dirt. Then Kino went to the fire where Juana was sitting.

At home, the doctor sat in his chair and looked at his watch. His servant brought him some chocolate and cakes. The doctor looked at the food, but he was not hungry.

In their houses, the neighbours talked about the pearl. They showed each other the size of the pearl. They told each other how beautiful the pearl was. The neighbours were watching to see how the pearl changed Kino and Juana. The neighbours all knew that the doctor had come because of the pearl.

The doctor's fat fingers put the pill far back on the baby's tongue.

The Doctor Comes

It was a hot night. The thin little dog came to Kino's door and looked in. The dog shook itself when Kino looked at it. When Kino looked away, the dog lay down. The dog did not enter the house, but it watched as Kino ate some food.

When Kino had finished his meal, Juana suddenly spoke.

'Kino,' she said.

Kino looked at Juana and then got up and went to her quickly. Kino could see that Juana was frightened. He stood over her and looked down. He could not see, because there was not enough light. Kino kicked some wood on the fire to make it burn. Soon he could see the baby's face. Coyotito's face was red and his lips were red. Suddenly, Coyotito's throat and stomach moved and he was very sick.

'So the doctor knew that the baby would be sick,' Kino said.

Kino remembered the medicine and he was sure that the doctor had made Coyotito sick. Juana moved from side to side and sang a little song. She thought that the song would keep away the danger. Coyotito moved about in Juana's arms and was suddenly sick again.

The doctor finished his chocolate and ate the little cakes. He brushed some little pieces of cake off his fingers and looked at his watch. Then he got up and took his bag.

The news about the baby's illness went quickly from house to house. Illness, like hunger, was the enemy of poor people. Some people said softly, 'Luck brings bad friends.' They all nodded their heads and got up to go to Kino's house. The

The Doctor Comes

neighbours walked quickly through the dark night until they were all in Kino's house again. They stood and talked about this illness that had come at a time of happiness. The old women sat down beside Juana to try and comfort her.

'All things are in God's hands,' they said.

The doctor came in, followed by his servant. The old women stood back quickly, as the doctor took the baby. The doctor then looked carefully at Coyotito and felt the baby's head.

'The poison is still there,' the doctor said. 'I think that I can make it go. I will do my best.'

The doctor asked for some water in a cup. He put some medicine in the cup and poured it into the baby's mouth. Coyotito coughed and cried and Juana watched with frightened eyes. The doctor spoke a little as he worked.

'It is lucky that I know about scorpion's poison,' he said.

Slowly, the baby stopped moving about in the doctor's arms. Then Coyotito breathed deeply and went to sleep, because the sickness had made him very tired. The doctor gave the baby back to Juana.

'He will get well now,' the doctor said. 'I have made him better.'

The doctor closed his bag and then spoke again.

'When do you think that you can pay the bill?' he asked.

'I will pay you when I have sold the pearl,' Kino replied.

'Have you got a pearl, a good pearl?' the doctor asked, with interest.

Then all the neighbours spoke together.

'He has found the greatest pearl in the world,' they said, and they showed the size of the pearl with their fingers.

The Doctor Comes

'Kino will be a rich man,' the neighbours said. 'No one has ever seen such a pearl.'

'I had not heard about it,' said the doctor, looking surprised. 'Do you keep this pearl in a safe place?' he asked. 'Perhaps you would like me to look after it for you?'

Kino looked at the doctor with half-shut eyes.

'I have put the pearl in a safe place,' he said. 'Tomorrow I will sell it, and then I will pay you.'

The doctor looked into Kino's eyes. He knew that the pearl would be somewhere in the house. He thought that Kino might look towards the place where the pearl was.

'It would be bad if the pearl was stolen before you could sell it,' the doctor said. And he saw that Kino's eyes looked quickly at the floor near the corner of the house.

When the doctor and the neighbours had gone, Kino sat by the fire and listened to the sounds of the night. Kino could hear the little waves on the beach and the barking of the dogs. He could hear the wind blowing through the roof and his neighbours talking in their houses. The fishermen do not sleep all night. They wake up from time to time, talk a little, then go to sleep again.

After a while, Kino got up and went to the door. He smelled the night air and listened for anyone coming. His eyes looked into the darkness because he was afraid. He was afraid that someone might come and steal the pearl. Kino went to the place in the corner where he had hidden the pearl. He took the pearl and brought it to his sleeping-mat. Kino made another little hole in the

The Doctor Comes

floor. He put his pearl in the hole and covered it up again.

Juana, who was sitting by the fire, watched Kino carefully.

'Who are you afraid of?' she asked.

'Everyone,' Kino replied.

After a while, Kino and Juana lay down together on the mat. Juana did not put Coyotito in his box that night. She held him in her arms and covered his face with her shawl. And the light went slowly out of the little fire.

But Kino was thinking while he was sleeping. He dreamt that Coyotito could read. In the dream he saw Coyotito reading from a book as large as a house. The letters in the book were as big as dogs. The dream ended and it was dark. Kino moved about on the mat. When Kino moved, Juana's eyes opened in the darkness. Then, Kino woke up and lay in the darkness, listening.

From the corner of the house came a soft noise. Kino could hear someone moving. He stopped breathing so that he could listen. He knew that the man in his house had stopped breathing, too. Kino thought that perhaps he had been dreaming. But Juana's hand touched him and he listened carefully. He heard the sound of breathing again. They could also hear the sound of someone's fingers in the dry earth.

Kino was suddenly angry. His hand went slowly to his knife. Then he jumped like an angry cat towards the corner of the house, with his knife in his hand. He felt someone's shirt and struck with his knife. He did not hit anything. Kino struck again and felt his knife going through the shirt. Then something hit Kino on the head. Kino's head

The Doctor Comes

was suddenly full of pain and he heard someone running towards the door. Then there was silence. Kino could feel warm blood running down his face and he could hear Juana calling to him.

'Kino! Kino!' she cried.
Juana sounded very frightened.
'I'm all right,' Kino said. 'He's gone.'

Kino went slowly back to his sleeping-mat. Juana was already working at the fire. She found a piece of burning ash and some little pieces of wood. Juana blew on the fire and made the flames burn. Soon a little light danced through the house. Then Juana took a candle, lit it from the flames and put the candle near the fire. Juana worked quickly, crying a little as she moved about. She put the end of her shawl in some water and washed the blood from Kino's head.

The Doctor Comes

'It's nothing,' Kino said, but his voice was hard and cold. Suddenly, Juana cried out.

'The pearl is bad!' she cried. 'It will destroy[16] us. Throw it away, Kino! Let's break the pearl with a big stone. Let's put the pearl in the ground. Let's throw the pearl back into the sea!'

In the firelight, Juana's lips and eyes looked very frightened. But Kino's face did not look frightened now.

'This is our one chance,' he said. 'Our son must go to school. Coyotito will not be a poor man. He will be free.'

'The pearl will destroy us,' Juana cried. 'The pearl will destroy our son, too.'

'Be quiet!' Kino cried. 'In the morning, we will sell the pearl. Be quiet, wife!'

Kino's dark eyes were angry as he looked into the little fire. His knife was still in his hands. Kino raised the knife and looked at it. He saw a little line of blood on it. Kino cleaned the knife by pushing it into the earth.

The morning wind blew on the water and through the trees. Little waves washed onto the sandy beach. Kino lifted up his sleeping-mat and found his pearl. He put the pearl in front of him and looked at it for a long time. The beauty of the pearl made Kino dream again. The pearl was so beautiful. The pearl would buy happiness for the future. The shining pearl would keep away illness and danger. Kino and Juana would never be hungry again.

As Kino looked at the pearl, the anger went out of his eyes and his face became softer. Juana looked at Kino and saw him smile. Juana smiled with him. And they began the new day with hope.

6
Kino Tries to Sell the Pearl

In the early morning, everyone knew that Kino was going to sell his pearl. Kino's neighbours and the fishermen from the little wooden houses knew. The shopkeepers knew about the pearl and people talked about it in church. The beggars knew that Kino was going to sell his pearl. The little boys were excited and the pearl buyers were excited too.

Each pearl buyer sat alone in his office. Each man played with a few pearls and thought about Kino. When someone wanted to sell a pearl, the buyers became very excited. The happiest pearl buyer was the buyer who bought pearls for the lowest prices. And all the buyers knew the price that they were going to offer Kino.

The sun was hot and yellow that morning. The canoes lay in a line on the beach, but the fishermen did not go out diving for pearls. They wanted to see Kino sell his pearl.

In the little wooden house by the sea, Kino's neighbours sat eating their breakfasts for a long time. They talked about the things they would do if they found the pearl. One man said that he would give all the money to the Church. Another man said that he would give all the money to the poor people in the town.

The neighbours hoped that the money would not change Kino. They hoped that Kino would not become greedy[17]. All the neighbours liked Kino and they did not want the pearl to destroy him.

'Kino has a good wife,' said the neighbours, 'and a beautiful baby. Kino and Juana will have more babies in

Kino Tries to Sell the Pearl

the future. We hope that the pearl will not destroy them all.'

For Kino and Juana, this morning was the most important morning of their lives. Coyotito was dressed in his best clothes. Juana combed her hair and tied the ends with two little bows of red ribbon. Then Juana put on her marriage skirt. Kino's clothes were old, but clean. This was the last day that Kino would wear old clothes. Tomorrow, or perhaps this afternoon, Kino would have new clothes.

The neighbours were dressed and ready, too. They were watching Kino's door. They were waiting for Kino and Juana to leave the house. Kino and Juana wanted the neighbours to come to the town, to watch Kino sell the pearl. Kino and Juana wanted their friends with them on this important day.

Juana put on her shawl carefully. She wrapped Coyotito in one end of the shawl so that the baby hung under her arm. Kino put on his big straw hat. He made sure that the hat was in the right place. Kino did not want the hat on the back or on the side of his head, like an unmarried man. He did not want the hat to be flat on his head, like an old man, either. Kino wanted the hat to be lifted a little at the front, to show that he was young and strong. People can tell many things by the way a man wears his hat.

Then Kino wrapped the great pearl in an old, soft piece of animal skin and put it in a little leather bag. He put the leather bag in his pocket. Kino folded his blanket over his left shoulder, and then he was ready.

Kino stepped out of the house. Juana followed, carrying Coyotito. As Kino and Juana walked up the little street towards the town, the neighbours came out of their houses. Many people and children came out of their houses. But because

Kino Tries to Sell the Pearl

the day was so important, only one man walked with Kino. That was Kino's brother, Juan Tomas.

'You must be careful that the buyers do not cheat[18] you,' Juan Tomas said.

'I shall be very careful,' Kino replied.

'How can we know what is a fair price[19]?' asked Juan Tomas. 'We do not know the price that the buyers give in other towns.'

'That is true,' Kino answered, 'but how can we know? We are here and we are not in the other towns!'

'Before you were born, Kino,' he said, 'the old people thought of a way to get more money for their pearls. The old people thought that if they paid a man to take all the pearls to the capital[20], he would get a better price.'

'I know,' Kino said, nodding his head. 'The idea was good.'

'The old people found a man to go to the capital,' Juan Tomas said. 'They gave all the pearls to the man and he went to the capital. But he never came back. Then they found another man and he went with the pearls and never came back. In the end, the people returned to the old way of selling pearls.'

'I know,' Kino said. 'I have heard our father talk about it. The idea was good, but it was against the teaching of the church. The priest said that each man and woman has been sent by God to guard some part of the world. We must all stay in our place and must not leave.'

'I have heard the priest say that,' Juan Tomas said. 'The priest says that every year.'

Kino had listened to the priest for many years. But the priest, like the doctor, was a man of a different race to Kino's people. This race had robbed and cheated Kino's people for

Kino Tries to Sell the Pearl

hundreds of years. Kino listened to what the priest said, but in his heart he did not believe him.

The line of people going to the town was quiet. The people knew that the day was very important. The neighbours did not allow their children to run or scream or play about. The day was so important that one old man came riding on his nephew's shoulders.

The line of people left the little wooden houses and came to the town. In the town, the streets were a little wider and there were narrow pavements beside the houses. As before, the beggars stood up and followed the people past the church. The shopkeepers closed their shops as their customers ran out to follow the crowd. The sun shone down on the streets and even the smallest stones made shadows on the ground.

The news of the crowd came to the pearl buyers in their dark little offices.

The offices had bars over the windows and were dark inside because the windows were very small. The buyers got ready for Kino. They put papers on their desks so that they could be at work when Kino came. The buyers put away their pearls, because a big pearl looked more valuable beside small pearls. The buyers knew that Kino's pearl was very big.

A fat man sat waiting in an office. The man's face looked kind and friendly. He was a man that said, 'Good morning!' to everyone. He always shook hands and told jokes. He always said nice things to please people, but he was not an honest man. This morning, the man had put a flower in a vase. He had put the vase beside the black cloth on his desk. He had shaved carefully and his hands were clean.

The buyer's door was open and he sang quietly as he played with a coin. The man played with the coin between his fingers

Kino Tries to Sell the Pearl

while he looked out of the door. He could hear the sound of feet coming. When Kino came in the door, the buyer quickly put the coin under the desk.

'Good morning, my friend,' the fat man said. 'What can I do for you?'

Kino had just come out of the bright sun and he could not see clearly in the dark office. The buyer still smiled, but his eyes had become hard. Under the desk, the buyer's left hand still played with the coin.

'I have a pearl,' Kino said.

Juan Tomas stood beside Kino and the neighbours were looking through the door. Some little boys were looking through Kino's legs.

'You have a pearl,' the buyer said. 'Sometimes a man brings me a dozen pearls. Let me see your pearl. I will value the pearl and give you a fair price.' And the buyer's fingers played faster and faster with the coin under the desk.

Kino slowly brought out the leather bag. He slowly took the soft piece of animal skin from the bag. Then, Kino put the great pearl onto the buyer's piece of black cloth. Kino looked at the buyer's face. The face did not change, but under the desk the buyer's fingers missed the coin and it dropped silently onto the floor. The buyer's right hand then touched the pearl on the black cloth. The buyer picked the pearl up between his fingers and looked at it closely.

Kino and his neighbours stopped breathing. The other people spoke very quietly.

'He's looking at the pearl,' they said. 'He has not said the price yet. They have not spoken about the price.'

The buyer put the pearl back on the black cloth. He pushed the pearl with his finger and smiled sadly.

'I will value the pearl and give you a fair price.'

Kino Tries to Sell the Pearl

'I'm sorry, my friend,' he said, and he lifted his shoulders a little, to show that he could do nothing.

'The pearl is very valuable,' Kino said.

The buyer's fingers pushed the pearl, so that it went from one side of the cloth to the other side.

'This pearl is too big,' the buyer said. 'Who would buy it? No one would buy such a pearl. I'm sorry.'

Kino did not understand.

'It is the greatest pearl in the world! Kino said. 'No one has ever seen such a pearl!'

'The pearl is big and interesting, but it is not valuable,' the buyer said. 'Perhaps I can give you a thousand pesos.'

Kino's face became dark and dangerous.

'The pearl is worth fifty thousand pesos,' he said. 'You know that is true and you want to cheat me!'

The buyer heard the people talking when they heard his price and the buyer felt a little afraid.

'I'm only one buyer,' the fat man said quickly. 'Go and ask the other buyers. Go to their offices and show your pearl to them. Or let the other buyers come here. Then you can see that we are not working together. Boy!'

The buyer's servant looked through the back door.

'Boy,' the buyer shouted, 'go to the other buyers. Ask the other buyers to come in here, but do not tell them the reason. Just say that I would be pleased to see them.'

The fat man put his hand under his desk and he began to play with a coin between his fingers again.

Kino's neighbours talked quietly together. They had been afraid that something was wrong with the pearl. The pearl was big, but it had a strange colour. The neighbours had thought about the colour from the moment that Kino had found

Kino Tries to Sell the Pearl

the pearl. A thousand pesos was not a bad price. A thousand pesos was a lot of money for a man who had no money at all. If Kino took the thousand, he would have a thousand more than before. Only yesterday Kino had nothing.

But Kino's face was hard and his lips were tight. Kino felt as if wild animals were all around him. He felt that everything was bad and that he was in danger. The great pearl shone on the black cloth and the buyer could not stop looking at it.

The people in the door stood back to let the three other buyers come in. The crowd was silent because the people wanted to see and hear everything. Kino was silent and careful. He felt someone pulling his shirt and he turned and looked into Juana's eyes. When Kino looked away, he felt strong again.

The buyers did not look at each other. They did not look at the pearl. The fat man spoke.

'I have given this man a price for this pearl,' he said. 'He does not think that my price is a fair price. I ask you to look at this – this thing – and give a price.

'Notice,' the fat man said to Kino. 'I have not told them my price.'

The first buyer was a thin little man. He looked at the pearl and took it between his fingers. Then he threw the pearl back on the black cloth.

'I will not give a price for this,' he said. 'I do not want it. This is not a real pearl!'

The second buyer was a little man with a soft voice. He took the pearl and looked at it carefully. The man took a glass from his pocket and looked at the pearl again. Then he laughed softly.

'Better pearls are made of plaster,' he said. 'I know these

Kino Tries to Sell the Pearl

things. This pearl is soft and it will lose its colour in a few months. Look.'

The man gave the glass to Kino. Kino had never seen a pearl through a glass before and he thought that his pearl looked very strange.

The third buyer took the pearl from Kino's hands.

'I know a man who likes such things,' the buyer said. 'I will give you five hundred pesos. Perhaps I can sell it to that man for six hundred.'

Kino quickly took the pearl from the third buyer. Kino placed the pearl in the piece of animal skin and put it in the little bag. The fat man behind the desk spoke.

'I'm a fool,' he said, 'but I will still give you one thousand pesos.'

Kino put the little bag into his pocket.

'What are you doing?' the fat man asked.

'You are cheating me!' Kino said angrily. 'My pearl is not for sale here. I will go to the capital.'

The buyers looked at each other quickly. The buyers knew that their prices were not high enough. They also knew that the rich buyer would be angry if they did not get the pearl. The fat man at the desk spoke again.

'Perhaps I could give you fifteen hundred pesos,' he said.

But Kino was pushing his way through the crowd. Kino's blood was beating in his ears as he pushed through the crowd and walked angrily away.

Juana ran after Kino down the street.

7
The Trouble Begins

When the evening came, the neighbours sat talking in their little wooden houses. No one had ever seen such a fine pearl before. They had thought that Kino's pearl was beautiful and valuable. But the buyers did not agree. And the buyers knew more about the price of pearls.

'The buyers did not talk to each other about the pearl,' the neighbours said. 'Each buyer said that the pearl had no value.'

'Do you think that the buyers talked about the pearl before?' one man asked.

'If that is true,' the others answered, 'then they have cheated us all our lives.'

Some of the neighbours said that Kino should have taken the fifteen hundred pesos. That was more money than Kino had ever seen. Perhaps Kino was a fool. Kino might go to the capital and find no buyer for his pearl. The buyers in the town would not give Kino the same price again.

Other people thought that Kino was a strong and brave man and that he was right.

'Good shall come to us all, because Kino is strong,' they said, and they were proud of Kino.

In his little house, Kino sat thinking on his sleeping-mat. He had put his pearl under a stone, near the fire. Kino felt afraid again. Kino had never been far from home in his life. He was afraid of strangers and strange places. He was very frightened of the capital, because it was so strange.

The capital was more than a thousand miles away, over the

The Trouble Begins

water and through the mountains. Every mile was strange and frightening. But Kino felt that his old world had gone and that he must find a new world. Kino's dream of the future was real and so he said, 'I will go.'

Juana looked at Kino while he put the pearl under the stone. Juana cleaned and fed Coyotito and made some corncakes for supper. Juan Tomas came in and sat down beside Kino. Juan Tomas did not speak for a long time. At last, Kino spoke.

'What could I do?' Kino said. 'The buyers were cheats!'

Juan Tomas nodded his head slowly. He was older than Kino and Kino wanted to know what his brother thought.

'I do not know the truth,' Juan Tomas said. 'We know that people cheat us all our lives, but we still live. You do not want to sell your pearl to the buyers. You want to change everything. I am afraid for you.'

'What have I to fear, except hunger?' Kino asked. But Juan Tomas shook his head slowly.

'We must all fear hunger,' Juan Tomas said. 'But even if your pearl is very valuable, do you think that you will get a fair price?'

'What do you mean?' Kino asked.

'I don't know,' Juan Tomas said, 'but I'm afraid for you. You are walking into a new world and you do not know the way.'

'I will go. I will go soon,' Kino said.

'Yes,' said Juan Tomas. 'You must go, but do you think you will find any different people in the capital? Here in the town, you have friends and you have me, your brother. In the capital, you will have no one.'

'What can I do?' Kino asked. 'The buyers have cheated us.

The Trouble Begins

My son must have a chance. The buyers are trying to cheat my son. My friends will help me.'

'Your friends will only help you if they are not in danger, too,' Juan Tomas said. Then he got up and said, 'Go with God.'

'Go with God,' Kino answered. But he did not look up, because his brother's words were strangely cold.

Long after Juan Tomas had gone, Kino sat thinking on his sleeping-mat. Kino felt tired and without hope. He did not know what to do. He could hear the sounds of the night. Juana looked at Kino. She knew that she could only help Kino by being silent and by being near to him. Juana was afraid, so she held Coyotito close and sang a little song to keep away the danger.

Kino did not move or ask for his supper. Juana knew that Kino would ask for the supper when he wanted to eat. Kino's eyes were still. He thought that he could hear something outside the house. Kino thought that something dark and bad was waiting for him outside in the night. The thing outside was dark and bad and it called Kino to come and fight. Kino's right hand went into his shirt and he felt his knife. His eyes were open wide. He stood up and went to the door.

Juana wanted to stop Kino. She lifted up her hand to stop him and her mouth opened. Kino looked out into the darkness for a long time and then he went outside. Juana heard something move through the air and hit Kino. Juana was too afraid to move for a moment. Then she pulled her lips back from her teeth like a cat.

She put Coyotito on the floor, took a stone from near the fire and ran outside. Kino lay on the ground.

Juana could not see anyone else. The only sound was the

Kino lay on the ground.

The Trouble Begins

sound of the wind and the waves. But Juana felt that someone was there in the darkness, behind the wooden fence or waiting in the shadow of the house.

Juana dropped her stone and put her arms around Kino. She helped him get up and walk into the house. Blood was running down Kino's face and he had a deep cut from his ear to his chin. Kino shook his head from side to side. His shirt and his clothes were torn. Juana helped Kino to his sleeping-mat and then she wiped the blood from his face with her skirt. She brought Kino some water to drink, but he still shook his head from side to side.

'Who was it?' Juana asked.

'I don't know,' Kino said. 'I didn't see.'

Juana washed the cut on Kino's face while he sat and looked in front of him.

'Kino, my husband,' Juana cried, and Kino's eyes looked past her. 'Can you hear me?' she asked.

'I can hear you,' Kino said, with a tired voice.

'Kino,' Juana said, 'This pearl is bad. Let's destroy it, before it destroys us! Let's break the pearl between two stones. Let's throw it back in the sea! Kino, the pearl is bad, it's bad!'

As Juana spoke, the light came back into Kino's eyes. His eyes shone with anger and his face became hard.

'No,' Kino said. 'I will fight. I will win! We will have our chance.'

And Kino hit his sleeping-mat with his hand.

'No one will take our good luck from us,' Kino said.

Kino looked at Juana. He did not seem so angry now. He put his hand on Juana's shoulder.

'Believe me,' he said, 'I am a man. In the morning, I will take our canoe and we will go over the sea and over the mountains to the capital. You will come with me. We will not be cheated. I am a man.'

'Kino,' Juana said, with a tired voice. 'I am afraid. Even a man can be killed. Let's throw the pearl back into the sea.'

And Juana was silent.

'Let's sleep a little,' Kino said. 'We will start when it is light. Are you afraid to go with me?'

'No, husband,' Juana answered.

Kino's eyes were soft and warm and his hand touched Juana's face.

'Let's sleep a little,' he said.

8

Fire and Death

Kino opened his eyes in the darkness. He felt something moving near him, but he did not move. Kino's eyes looked into the darkness. The light of the moon came through the holes in the little house.

By the light of the moon, Kino saw Juana get up silently. He saw her go towards the fireplace. Kino heard a little sound as Juana moved the stone. Then she went quietly to the door. She stopped for a moment, near Coyotito's hanging box. Then Kino saw Juana in the doorway as she went out.

Kino was very angry. He got up and quickly followed Juana. Kino could hear her footsteps going towards the sea. Kino's

Fire and Death

anger was burning in his head as he silently followed her. Juana went through some bushes and over some stones towards the water. Then she heard Kino coming and she started to run.

Juana's arm was up and ready to throw the pearl into the sea. Kino jumped forward and held her arm and took the pearl.

Then Kino hit Juana in the face with his hand. Juana fell on the stones and Kino kicked her as she lay on the ground. In the moonlight, Kino could see the little waves washing over Juana. Her skirt floated around her legs in the water.

Kino looked down and angrily showed his teeth. Juana

Fire and Death

looked up with wide, frightened eyes. Juana was like a sheep in front of a butcher. She knew that Kino could kill her and she would not stop him. Juana was waiting for death. Then the anger left Kino and he felt sick at what Juana had done. Kino could not think clearly any more. He turned away and walked back through the bushes.

Suddenly, he heard someone running at him. Kino struck with his knife and he felt the knife go in. Then someone pulled Kino to the ground and Kino felt greedy fingers going into his pockets. The pearl dropped onto the little stone pathway and shone in the moonlight.

Juana pulled herself up from the water. Her face and the side of her body were full of pain. She pulled herself up onto her knees. Juana was not angry with Kino. She needed Kino and she could not live without him. Juana did not understand Kino very well, but she knew him and needed him. Of course Juana would follow Kino. She would follow Kino, because she might be able to save him.

Juana got up slowly. She washed her face with the sea water and then went slowly up the beach after Kino. Some clouds had moved over the sky from the south. The moon went in and out of the clouds so that Juana sometimes walked in darkness and sometimes in the moonlight. Her back was bent with pain and her head hung low. She went through the bushes when the moon was covered with clouds. When it was light again, Juana saw the great pearl shining on the stone pathway. She knelt down and took the pearl.

The moon went behind a cloud again. Juana stayed on her knees and thought about going back to the sea again. When the moon came out from behind the clouds, Juana saw two men lying on the path in front of her. Juana jumped up and saw that

She knelt down and took the pearl.

Fire and Death

---

one of the men was Kino. The other man was a stranger. The stranger had blood coming from his throat.

Kino moved a little and tried to talk. His arms and legs moved slowly, like the legs of a half-dead animal. A dead man was lying on the path and Kino's knife was lying next to the dead man. And Kino's knife was covered with blood. Juana wanted to live the old life, the life before the pearl. But their lives had changed since they found the pearl. Bad things had happened. And now, Kino had killed a man. Now, Kino and Juana could do nothing except run away.

Juana's pain had gone now. She quickly pulled the dead man from the pathway, into the bushes. Juana went to Kino and washed his face with her wet skirt. At last, Kino spoke.

'They have taken the pearl,' he said. 'I have lost the pearl. My dream is finished. The pearl has gone.'

Juana comforted Kino as she would comfort a sick child.

'Here is your pearl,' Juana said. 'I found the pearl on the path. Can you hear me now? Here is your pearl. Can you understand? You have killed a man. We must go away. People will come for us. Don't you understand? We must go, before daylight comes.'

'Someone attacked me,' Kino answered. 'I hit him to save my life.'

'Do you think anyone will believe that?' Juana asked.

'No,' Kino answered, breathing deeply. 'You are right!'

Kino became a strong man again.

'Go to our house and bring Coyotito,' Kino said. 'Bring all the corn that we have. I will push the canoe into the water and we will go.

Kino took his knife and left Juana. Kino ran towards the beach and he came to his canoe. By the light of the moon, he

Fire and Death

saw a big hole in the bottom of his boat. Kino was so angry that he felt even stronger than before. His grandfather's canoe had been built with strong plaster. Now, it had a big hole in the bottom.

The killing of a boat was something very bad for the fishermen. The killing of a man was not so bad as the killing of a boat. A boat does not have sons and a boat cannot fight. A wounded boat does not get better.

Kino was angry and sad, but now he was as strong as an animal.

Now, Kino lived only to hide and to fight. He lived only to fight for his family. He ran up the beach and through the bushes to his little house.

The cockerels were crowing now and it was getting light. Smoke from the first fires was coming out of the houses. Kino could smell breakfast cooking. The early birds were moving in the bushes. The moon was losing its light and the clouds were getting thicker in the south. The wind blew and Kino could smell rain in the air.

Kino suddenly felt happy as he hurried to his house. He would think clearly because now he had only one thing to do. He had to go away. Kino touched the great pearl in his shirt. Then he felt his knife hanging round his neck.

Suddenly, Kino saw a little light in front of him, and then a tall flame jumped into the air. The flame made a loud noise as it lit up the pathway. Kino started to run because he knew that his house was burning. Kino also knew that these little wooden houses could burn down in a few minutes.

As Kino ran, Juana came running towards him with Coyotito in her arms. The baby was crying and Juana's eyes were wide and frightened. Kino could see what had

Fire and Death

happened. He did not ask Juana any questions. Kino knew what had happened before Juana spoke.

'Some men were in the house,' Juana said. 'They were looking for the pearl. Then they set fire to the wood.'

The strong light from the burning house shone on Kino's face.

'Who was it?' Kino asked.

'I don't know,' Juana answered. 'I could not see.'

The neighbours came running out of their houses. People tried to stop pieces of burning wood falling onto the other little houses.

Suddenly, Kino was afraid. The light made him afraid. Kino remembered the dead man in the bushes near the path. He took Juana's arm and pulled her into the shadow of the house. He did not want the neighbours to see them. Kino pulled Juana away from the light because light was now a danger to them.

Kino and Juana went quickly to the house of Juan Tomas. Kino went in the door and pulled Juana after him. Outside, Kino and Juana could hear the cries of children and the shouts of the neighbours. The neighbours thought that Kino might be inside the burning house.

9
Kino and Juana Run Away

The house of Juan Tomas was almost the same as Kino's house. Nearly all the little wooden houses were the same. All the houses were full of holes and Juana and Kino could still see the flames through the wall. They could see the tall flames burning up and they saw the roof of their house fall in.

Then Juana and Kino heard the shouts of their friends and the loud, high cry of Apolonia, the wife of Juan Tomas. Apolonia began to cry, like all the women cried when someone died in the family. A few minutes later, Apolonia came into her house to get her shawl. As she looked in a box by the wall, Kino spoke very quietly.

'Apolonia,' Kino said, 'don't cry out. We are here.'

'How did you get here?' Apolonia asked.

'Don't ask any questions now,' Kino answered. 'Go to Juan Tomas and bring him here and don't tell the others. This is very important, Apolonia.'

Apolonia looked at Kino.

Kino and Juana Run Away

'Yes, Kino,' she said.

In a few moments Juan Tomas came back with his wife. Juan Tomas lit a candle and came to Kino and Juana in the corner.

'Apolonia,' Juan Tomas said. 'Go to the door and don't let anyone come in.'

Juan Tomas was older than Kino and he seemed to know what to do.

'Now brother,' Juan Tomas said. 'Tell me what happened.'

'Someone attacked me in the dark,' Kino said. 'And in the fight I killed a man.'

'Who?' Juan Tomas asked quickly.

'I don't know,' Kino answered. 'It was dark – very dark.'

'The man wanted the pearl,' Juan Tomas said. 'That pearl is bad, Kino. You should have sold the pearl. Perhaps you can still sell it.'

'Brother,' Kino said. 'Something very bad has happened. Something has happened that is worse than death. Someone has made a hole in my canoe and burnt my house. A dead man is in the bushes. Men are watching and waiting to kill me. You must hide us, brother.'

Kino looked at his brother closely and he saw that Juan Tomas was afraid of the danger.

'We don't need to hide here for a long time,' Kino said.

'I will hide you,' Juan Tomas answered.

'I do not want to bring danger to you,' Kino said. 'I will go tonight and then you will be safe.'

'I will help you,' said Juan Tomas, and he called to Apolonia.

'Apolonia, close the door,' he said. 'Don't tell anyone that Kino and Juana are here.'

Kino and Juana Run Away

Kino and Juana sat silently, all day, in the darkness of the house. They could hear the neighbours speaking. Through the walls of the house, Kino and Juana could see the neighbours. Kino and Juana heard their neighbours talking about their broken boat. Juan Tomas went out to talk to the neighbours. He did not tell the neighbours what had happened to Kino, Juana and the baby.

'I think that they have gone south along the coast,' Juan Tomas said to one man. To another man he said, 'Kino would never leave the sea. Perhaps he found another boat.' And then Juan Tomas said, 'Apolonia is ill with sadness.'

That day, the wind blew strongly over the sea and the bushes along the coast. The wind blew strongly through the little wooden houses and no boat was safe in the water.

'Kino will have drowned if he went to sea,' the neighbours said.

Every time Juan Tomas went to see his neighbours, he came back with something for Kino and Juana. Juan Tomas brought a little bag of red beans and some rice. He brought a cup of dried peppers and some salt, and he brought a long, heavy knife. Kino's eyes shone when he saw the knife. Kino touched the knife and it felt very sharp.

The wind blew strongly over the sea and made the water white. The trees moved about like frightened animals. Sand blew up from the land and made a cloud over the sea. The wind blew away the clouds and made the sky clear and clean. In the evening, Juan Tomas talked to his brother.

'Where will you go?' Juan Tomas asked Kino.

'To the north,' Kino answered. 'I have heard that there are cities in the north.'

'Don't go near the beach,' said Juan Tomas. 'People are

searching along the beach. The men in the town are looking for you. Have you still got the pearl?'

'Yes, I have,' Kino answered. 'And I will keep it.' And Kino's eyes were hard and cruel[21].

Coyotito cried a little and Juana sang quietly to make him silent.

'The wind is good,' said Juan Tomas. 'The wind will blow away your tracks[22].'

Kino and Juana left quietly in the dark, before the moon came up. The family stood in the house of Juan Tomas. Juana carried Coyotito on her back. She carried Coyotito in her shawl and the baby slept with one cheek against Juana's shoulder. One end of the shawl covered Juana's nose and kept away the cold night air. Juan Tomas kissed Kino on both cheeks.

'Go with God,' Juan Tomas said. 'Why don't you throw away the pearl?'

'The pearl has become my life,' Kino answered. 'If I throw away the pearl, I shall lose my life. Go also with God, Juan Tomas.'

The strong wind blew sticks and sand and little stones through the air. Kino and Juana covered their faces as they walked along. The wind had cleared the dark sky and the stars shone brightly. Kino and Juana walked carefully. They did not go into the town because they did not want anyone to see them. Kino and Juana went past the town and turned north. They followed the sandy road that led through the forest to the next town.

Kino could feel the sand blowing against his legs. He was happy because he knew that the sand would blow away the tracks. He could see the narrow road through the forest by

Kino and Juana Run Away

the light of the stars. Kino could hear the sound of Juana's feet. Kino went quickly and Juana was almost running behind.

Kino's people had always been afraid of the night and Kino was afraid, too. Kino was like a hunted animal now. He moved quickly and carefully. The wind made a frightening noise through the trees and bushes, as Kino and Juana walked on through the darkness. At last, the moon came up on their right. When the moon came up, the wind stopped and the air was still again.

Kino and Juana could see the little road in front of them. The sandy road was deeply cut with wheel tracks. Now that the wind had stopped, Kino and Juana would also leave tracks.

Kino and Juana walked all night without stopping. In the early morning, Kino looked for a place to hide during the day. He found a place near the road. An animal had made a place in the bushes. No one could see the place from the road. Juana sat down and fed the baby and Kino went back to the road. Kino broke off a piece of tree and carefully swept away the tracks.

It was getting light now. Kino heard a cart coming along the road. Kino bent down near the road and watched a heavy, two-wheel cart go by. When the cart had gone, Kino went back to the road and looked at the cart tracks. Kino saw that his tracks had gone. He swept the ground again and then went back to Juana.

Juana gave Kino some corncakes that Apolonia had made. Juana then slept a little, while Kino sat and looked at the ground.

The hot sun came up in the sky. Kino and Juana were not near the sea now, and the air was very dry and hot. Kino could smell the trees in the hot air. Juana woke up when the sun was high in the sky. Then Kino pointed at the trees.

Kino heard a cart coming along the road.

Kino and Juana Run Away

'Be careful of that tree there,' Kino said to Juana. 'Do not touch the tree. If you touch it and then touch your eyes, you will become blind.'

Then Kino pointed to another tree.

'Do not break the branch of that tree,' he said. 'If you break the branch, red blood will run out, and the blood brings bad luck.'

Juana nodded and smiled a little because she knew these things.

'Will they follow us?' Juana asked. 'Do you think that they will try to find us?'

'They will try,' Kino answered. 'If they find us, they will take the pearl. Oh, yes, they will try.'

Then Juana said, 'Perhaps the buyers were right and the pearl has no value. Perhaps we are wrong.'

Kino put his hand in his pocket and brought out the pearl. The sun made the pearl shine brightly.

'No,' Kino said, 'they would not have tried to steal the pearl if it was not valuable.'

'Do you know who attacked you?' Juana asked. 'Was it the buyers?'

'I don't know,' Kino answered. 'I didn't see the people who attacked me.'

Kino looked into the pearl and started to dream again. He tried to dream of all the things that he wanted. But he could not dream again. He could only think of the terrible things that had happened since they found the pearl.

'When we sell this pearl, I will have a rifle,' he said.

Kino tried to think about the rifle, but he could only think of death. He thought of the man that he had killed with his knife.

'We will be married in the church,' Kino said quickly.

But when Kino tried to think about his marriage, he thought about Juana. He could only think of the blood on Juana's face where he had hit her.

Kino was afraid, but he spoke again.

'Our son must learn to read,' he said.

Kino looked at his pearl and he tried to dream of his son reading a book. But instead, Kino dreamt about the doctor who had made Coyotito sick.

Kino stopped thinking about these terrible things and he put the pearl back into his pocket.

10
The Trackers

The sun was so hot that Kino and Juana moved into the shade of the bushes. Small birds moved about in the shade. Kino covered his eyes with his hat and wrapped his blanket around his face to keep the flies off. Then he slept.

But Juana did not sleep. Her face was still full of pain because Kino had hit her. Big flies flew around the cut on Juana's chin. When Coyotito woke up, Juana put him on the ground and watched the baby wave his arms and kick his feet. Coyotito smiled at Juana and Juana smiled, too. Juana played with Coyotito and gave him some water to drink.

Kino was dreaming in his sleep. He moved about and cried

The Trackers

out in a loud voice. Kino's hands moved as if he was fighting. Suddenly, he sat up. He was breathing deeply.

Kino listened, but he heard only the sounds of the forest.

'What's the matter?' Juana asked.

'Quiet!' Kino answered.

'You are only dreaming,' Juana said.

'Perhaps,' Kino replied.

Kino could not sleep again. When Juana gave him a corncake, Kino stopped eating to listen. Kino was afraid. He looked over his shoulder into the trees and held his knife firmly in his hand. Coyotito made a little noise and Kino said, 'Keep him quiet!'

'What's the matter?' Juana asked again.

'I don't know,' Kino answered.

Suddenly, he saw something moving. Kino bent his head down and looked through the trees. Far away, Kino could see three men. Two of the men were walking and the other man was riding a horse. Kino knew what the men were doing. Suddenly, Kino felt very frightened. The men who were walking were carefully looking at the ground. One of the men stopped and pointed at something. Kino knew that the men were trackers.

These trackers could follow the tracks of sheep in the rocky mountains. They could see a piece of broken grass or little marks in the sand. They were as clever as hunting dogs. The man on the horse had a blanket covering his nose. He was carrying a rifle in his hand.

Kino stood as still as a tree. He almost stopped breathing. His eyes looked at the place where he had swept away the tracks. The marks of the sweeping might tell the trackers

Kino bent his head down and looked through the trees.

The Trackers

something. Kino knew these men. They were very clever hunters and now they were hunting Kino.

Suddenly, the trackers saw something and they bent over to look more closely. The man on the horse waited and watched. The trackers made a noise like excited dogs. Kino slowly pulled out his knife and got ready. He knew what he must do. If the trackers found Kino, then he must jump at the horseman. He must kill the horseman quickly and take the rifle. That was Kino's only chance. As the men came nearer, Kino got ready.

Juana could hear the horse coming. The baby made a little noise. Juana took Coyotito and put him under her shawl and fed him.

When the trackers came near, Kino could only see their legs and the legs of the horse through the trees. Kino could see the men's dirty feet and their old clothes. The trackers came nearer and stopped again. The horseman stopped, too. The horse moved its head up and down and breathed loudly through its nose. Then the trackers turned and looked at the horse and watched the animal's ears. They wanted to see if the horse could hear any strange noises.

Kino stopped breathing and his arms and legs were ready to fight. The trackers bent over the road for a long time. Then they moved away slowly. They looked at the ground all the time and the horseman followed behind. The trackers ran a little, stopped to look at the ground and then ran again. Kino knew that they would come back. They would look and stop and then look again until they had found Kino's tracks.

Kino went back into the forest. He did not cover his tracks. He could not cover his tracks because he had broken too many bushes and had moved too many stones. Kino was so

The Trackers

frightened now that he wanted to run away. He knew that the hunters would find his tracks. He must take Juana and Coyotito and run away as fast as possible. Kino went back to Juana silently and quickly. As he came near, Juana looked up.

'Trackers,' Kino said, 'Come on!'

Then Kino suddenly felt that all hope had gone.

'Perhaps I should let the trackers find me,' he said.

Juana jumped up and put her hand on Kino's arm.

'You have the pearl,' she said. 'Do you think that those men would take you back to the town alive?'

Kino's hand went slowly to his pocket.

'They will find the pearl,' he said quietly.

'Come on!' Juana said, 'Come on!'

When Kino did not move, Juana spoke again.

'Do you think that they would not kill me, too?' she asked. 'Do you think that they would not kill Coyotito?'

Juana had made Kino think. Kino's lips were tight over his teeth and his eyes were full of hate and anger.

'Come on,' he said. 'We will go to the mountains. Perhaps we can hide in the mountains.'

Kino picked up the little bags of food and the water-bottle in his left hand. In his right hand he carried his big knife. Juana followed Kino through the bushes and they went quickly towards the high mountains. They walked quickly through the bushes. Kino was so frightened that he did not cover the tracks. They walked quickly, kicking the stones and breaking the leaves from the trees. Kino and Juana could see the high mountains rising out of the forest and standing against the sky. They ran towards the mountains like hunted animals.

This land had no water. Kino and Juana walked on broken stones and little pieces of dry grass. This desert country was

The Trackers

burning hot. In front, the rocky mountains looked cool and safe.

Kino walked as fast as he could. He knew what would happen. The hunters would soon find the tracks. Then they would come to the place where Kino and Juana had slept. The trackers could easily follow, because of the broken stones and fallen leaves. They would find Kino and Juana. They would not take Kino and Juana and Coyotito back to the town. The horseman had a rifle.

The little path became steeper and the stones were larger. But now Kino and his family were a long way from the trackers. Kino and Juana stopped to rest. Kino climbed onto a big rock and looked back. He could not see the trackers. Kino could not even see the tall horseman riding through the bushes.

Juana sat in the shade of the rock. She put the water-bottle to Coyotito's lips and he drank the water quickly. Kino climbed down from the large rock and looked at Juana. He saw that her feet were cut from the stones and bushes. Juana quickly covered her feet with her skirt. Then Juana gave the water-bottle to Kino, but he shook his head. He was thirsty, but there was only a little water left.

'Juana,' said Kino. 'I will go and you will hide. I will go to the mountains and the trackers will follow me. When they have gone, you will go north. Then, I will come to you.'

Juana looked into Kino's eyes for a moment.

'No,' she said. 'We will go with you.'

'I can go faster alone,' Kino said angrily. 'You will put Coyotito in more danger if you go with me.'

'No,' Juana said.

'You must,' Kino answered. 'I want you to hide.'

'No,' Juana said again.

The Trackers

Kino looked at Juana. He could see no fear or weakness in her face. Juana's eyes were very bright and they seemed to make Kino strong. When Kino and Juana started walking again, he was no longer frightened.

Kino and Juana climbed higher towards the mountains. They were walking on flat rocks now and they were not making tracks. Kino knew that when the hunters lost his tracks, they must search until they found the tracks again. So Kino did not go straight to the mountains. He wanted to make it more difficult for the trackers to find them. Sometimes he left the rocks and made tracks in other places. Then he went back to the rocks and climbed up the mountain to Juana. The path went up and up and Kino and Juana breathed heavily as they walked.

The sun was going slowly down as Kino and Juana walked into a valley. The valley was dark and full of shadows. Kino could see some little bushes in the valley. The water-bottle was empty now and Kino thought that he might find water near the bushes. But the valley was dangerous because the trackers would also want water.

Kino was right. There was a pool near the bushes. A stream ran down from the cold snow at the top of the mountain and made a large pool. Bushes and tall grass grew beside the pool. There was a small, sandy beach which was full of the tracks of animals that had come to drink water.

The sun had gone over the mountain when Kino and Juana came at last to the water. From the pool, they could look across to the sea far away. Kino and Juana were both very tired. Juana fell to her knees and washed Coyotito's face. Then she filled the bottle and gave the baby a drink.

Kino was very thirsty and drank for a long time from the

The Trackers

pool. Then he lay beside the water and watched Juana feeding the baby. When Kino had rested, he stood up. From the pool, Kino looked down the side of the mountain. Kino suddenly saw something and he stood very still. He could see the trackers far down the bottom of the mountain. They were far away and looked very small.

Juana had turned to look at Kino and she saw him standing still.

'How far?' she asked quietly.

'They will be here by evening,' Kino answered.

Kino looked up the valley, where the water was coming down.

'We must climb higher,' he said, looking up at the rocky hill above the pool.

11
The Cry of Death

While Kino was looking up, he saw some caves. The caves were about thirty feet up on the rocky hill. Kino climbed up, holding the rocks with his hands and feet. The caves were a few feet deep and made by the wind. Kino crawled into the largest cave and lay down. He knew that nobody could see him from outside. He crawled out of the cave again and climbed quickly down to Juana.

'We must go up there,' Kino said. 'Perhaps the men will not find us up there.'

Juana did not ask Kino any questions. She filled her water-bottle to the top and Kino helped her up to the cave. Kino brought up the packages of food and passed them to Juana. She sat in the entrance of the cave and watched.

Juana saw that Kino did not try to rub out their tracks in the sand. Instead, Kino climbed up the rocks beside the water and pulled out the little plants.

When Kino had climbed a hundred feet, he slowly came down again. He looked carefully at the rocks leading to the cave. He saw that there were no marks. Then he climbed up to the cave and crawled in beside Juana.

'The trackers will see these marks I have made and they will follow them,' said Kino. 'When the men go up there, we will go back down again. But I am afraid that the baby will cry. You must not let the baby cry.'

'He will not cry,' Juana said.

She lifted the baby and looked into Coyotito's eyes. Coyotito looked at Juana.

The Cry of Death

'He knows not to cry,' she said.

Kino lay in the entrance of the cave. He watched the shadow of the mountain move across the land until the shadow reached the sea. Then all of the land was in the shadow.

Kino and Juana waited a long time. The trackers did not come to the little pool until the evening. The three men were on foot because the horse could not climb the side of the hill. From the cave, the men looked like little people. Two of the trackers moved about on the small beach, near the pool. They saw Kino's tracks going up the mountain. The man with the rifle sat down and rested. The other two men sat down, too. Kino could see the light of their cigarettes. Kino could see the men eating and he could hear their voices.

Night came to the valley. The animals that drank from the pool came near. The animals smelt the men and went away again into the darkness. Kino heard a sound behind him. Juana was whispering, 'Coyotito'. She was telling the baby to be quiet. Kino saw Juana cover Coyotito's head with her shawl.

Down on the beach, one of the men lit a match. Kino saw that the other two men were sleeping. They looked like sleeping dogs. The third man watched. Kino could see the man's rifle by the light of the match. The match went out, but Kino still knew where the men were. In his mind, Kino could see the two men sleeping and the third man with his rifle between his knees.

Kino moved quietly back into the cave. Juana's eyes were like two bright stars. Kino crawled close to Juana and put his lips near her face.

'There is a way to fight them,' he said.

'But they will kill you,' Juana answered.

From the cave, the men looked like little people.

The Cry of Death

'If I can get to the man with the rifle, I shall be all right,' Kino replied. 'The other two men are sleeping.'

Juana's hand came out from under her shawl and held Kino's arm.

'The men will see your white clothes in the starlight,' Juana said.

'No, they won't see me in the starlight,' Kino answered, 'but I must go before the moon rises.'

Kino tried to think of something kind to say.

'If the men kill me,' he said, 'stay here quietly. When they have gone away, go back home.'

Juana's voice shook as she said, 'Go with God.'

Kino looked closely at Juana and he could see her large eyes. Kino put out his hand and found Coyotito. For a moment, Kino put his hand on the baby's head. Then Kino raised his hand and touched Juana's face. Juana held her breath as Kino crawled out of the cave.

Kino stood in the entrance of the cave for a moment and Juana could see him against the sky. He was taking off his white clothes. The men would not see Kino's brown skin in the darkness. Kino hung his big knife around his neck so that his hands were free. Juana could see Kino in the cave entrance. He did not come back to her. Kino was bending forward and looking. Then, suddenly, he disappeared.

Juana crawled to the entrance of the cave and looked out. She was like a bird looking out of its hole in the mountain. Coyotito was asleep under the blanket on Juana's back. His head was resting against Juana's neck and shoulder. Juana was quietly whispering her prayers.

When Juana looked out of the cave, the night seemed less dark. The sky was getting light in the east. Juana looked

The Cry of Death

down and she could see the burning cigarette of the man with the gun.

Kino went slowly down the rocks. He hung his knife down his back, so that the knife would not hit against the stone. Kino climbed down the mountain with his fingers and toes and he pressed himself against the rocks so that he would not fall. Any sound, like a little stone rolling down the rocks, would wake the men below. Any unusual sound would make the man with the rifle look up. But the night was not so silent. The noise of insects filled the valley.

Kino went slowly and silently down the mountain. One foot moved a few inches and then his toes held on to the stone. The other foot moved and then one hand went a little downwards. Then the other hand went down, until Kino's whole body had moved very slowly. Kino's mouth was open so that even his breath would make no sound.

If the men below heard a sound and looked up, they would see Kino's body against the rocks. Kino had to move very slowly, so as not to make the men look up. The climb down took a long time. When Kino reached the bottom, he hid behind a little tree. Kino's heart was beating quickly and his hands and face were wet with sweat[23]. He bent down and breathed deeply.

The men were only twenty feet away. Kino tried to remember what the ground was like. He tried to remember if there were any big stones in the way. Kino rubbed his legs because they were shaking after the climb down. Then Kino looked towards the east. The moon was going to rise in a few moments and he must attack before it rose.

It was now getting lighter in the valley. Kino could see the men who were sleeping. First, he had to kill the watcher

The Cry of Death

quickly. Silently, Kino pulled his knife over his shoulder and held the handle. But Kino was too late. As he stood up, the moon appeared in the east. Kino bent down again behind the little tree.

It was now getting lighter in the valley. Kino could see the watcher sitting on the little hill near the pool. The watcher was looking at the moon. He lit another cigarette and the match shone in his face for a moment. Kino could not wait any longer. When the watcher turned his head, Kino must jump. His legs were ready. And then, from above him, came a little cry. The watcher turned his head to listen and then stood up. One of the sleepers moved on the ground. This man sat up and looked around.

'What is it?' asked the man who had woken up.

'You can't tell,' said the man who had been asleep. 'Perhaps it is a wild dog with some puppies[24]. I've heard a puppy cry like a baby.'

The sweat rolled down Kino's face and fell into his eyes and burnt them. The little cry came again and the watcher looked up the side of the hill to the dark cave.

'Perhaps there's a wild dog up there,' said the watcher.

Kino heard a movement as the man got ready to shoot his rifle.

'If it's a wild dog, this will stop it,' said the watcher. And he raised his rifle towards the cave.

Kino jumped forward as the rifle fired. Kino's large knife swung and cut through the man's neck and chest. Kino was a terrible killer now. He took the rifle with one hand. With the other, he pulled his knife out of the man's body.

The Cry of Death

Kino moved very fast. He turned round and hit the second man's head. The third man crawled away, into the pool. Then he began to climb up the rocks where the water came down. The man's hands and feet were caught in the bushes. He cried as he tried to climb up. But Kino had become hard and cruel. He raised the rifle and fired. Kino saw the man fall backwards into the pool. Kino walked into the water. In the moonlight, he could see the man's frightened eyes. Then Kino fired the rifle, between the man's eyes.

Kino stood and looked up to the cave. Something was wrong. The insects were silent now. Kino listened. He knew the sound. He knew the long, rising cry from the little cave in the side of the mountain. He knew it was Juana's voice. The sound was the cry of death.

12
Kino and Juana Return Home

Everyone in the town remembers the return of Kino and Juana. Some old people saw them come back. Other people were told by their fathers and grandfathers a long time later. But everyone remembers the day.

Late one afternoon, some little boys ran into the town with the news. Everyone came out of their houses to see Kino and Juana. The sun was going down and the shadows on the ground were long. Everyone remembers Kino and Juana and the long, black shadows.

Kino and Juana came from the sandy road into the town. Kino was not walking in front of Juana. They were walking side by side. The sun was behind them and their long shadows were in front. Kino had a rifle in his hand and Juana carried her shawl over her shoulder like a heavy bag. The shawl had blood on it.

Juana's face was hard and covered with lines because she was so tired. Her wide open eyes seemed to see nothing. Kino's lips were thin and his mouth was shut tight. People say that

Kino and Juana Return Home

Kino looked as dangerous as a wild animal that day. The crowd of people pushed back as Kino and Juana passed.

Kino and Juana walked through the town, but they did not see anything. Their eyes did not look to the right or to the left. They did not look up or down. They only looked ahead.

Kino and Juana walked side by side, through the town and down to the little wooden houses. The neighbours stood back to let Kino and Juana pass. Juan Tomas lifted up his hand, but he said nothing and left his hand in the air.

Kino and Juana walked past their burnt house, but they did not look at it. They walked through the bushes and went down to the water. They did not look towards Kino's broken canoe. When Kino and Juana came to the water, they stopped and looked at the sea. Then Kino put the rifle down, put his hand in his pocket and took out the large pearl.

Kino looked and remembered all the terrible things that had happened. In the pearl, Kino saw cruel faces and flames burning up. He saw the frightened eyes of the man in the pool. Kino saw Coyotito lying in the cave with blood on his head. And the pearl looked bad and ugly.

Kino's hand shook a little as he turned slowly to Juana. He held the pearl out to her. Juana was still holding Coyotito's dead body over her shoulder. She looked at the pearl in Kino's hand for a moment. Then she looked into Kino's eyes and said quietly, 'No, you must do it.'

Kino lifted up his arm and threw the pearl as far as he could. Kino and Juana watched the pearl shining in the evening sun. They saw the pearl drop into the sea. They stood side by side for a long time, watching the movement on the water.

The surface of the sea was like a green mirror. The pearl went down into the beautiful, green water and dropped

Kino and Juana Return Home

towards the bottom of the sea. The pearl went down through the seaweed and fell among the plants in the sand. The pearl lay on the floor of the sea. And the pearl was gone.

Points for Understanding

1

1 What happened to Coyotito?
2 Who did Juana want bringing for the baby?

2

1 How did the beggars know that Kino and Juana were poor?
2 How was Kino going to pay the doctor?
3 Why did Kino hit the doctor's gate with his hand?

3

1 Why was a canoe valuable?
2 What was Juana praying for?
3 Where did the oysters live?
4 What did Kino find in the big oyster?
5 What did the seaweed do to Coyotito's wound?

4

1 Why did Kino become everyone's enemy?
2 What three things did Kino dream of when he held the pearl in his hands?
3 Why did the pearl make Kino happy?
4 Why did Kino become afraid?

5

1 Why did the doctor come to see Coyotito?
2 Kino didn't like the doctor. Why did he let the doctor into the house?
3 Why did Juana want to destroy the pearl?
4 What was Kino going to do the next morning?

6

1 Did the buyers offer Kino a fair price for the pearl?
2 What did Kino decide to do with the pearl?

7

1 Why did Juan Tomas think that Kino should not go to the capital?
2 What happened when Kino went outside his house?
3 What did Juana want Kino to do with the pearl?
4 What was Kino's reply to Juana?

8

1 Why did Kino hit Juana?
2 Why did Kino and Juana have to run away?
3 Why could Kino no longer go across the sea to the capital?
4 What happened to Kino's house?
5 Where did Kino and Juana hide?

9

1 Why did Kino sweep the ground behind him?
2 Why didn't Kino and Juana keep walking during the day?
3 What happened when Kino tried to dream of:
   (a) having a rifle?
   (b) marriage in church?
   (c) Coyotito learning to read?

10

1 Who were the three men on the road?
2 What was the man on the horse carrying?
3 What must Kino do if the trackers found them?
4 Why was Kino still afraid, although the trackers had gone past them?
5 Why did Kino want to go to the mountains alone?
6 What did Kino find in the valley?
7 Why did Kino want to leave the pool and climb higher?

11

1 Where did Kino and Juana hide?
2 What did Kino decide to do?
3 Why did the man by the pool fire his rifle?
4 How did Kino know that something terrible had happened to Coyotito?

12

1 What was in the shawl on Juana's shoulder?
2 What did Kino do with the pearl?

Glossary

1. ***the cockerels were beginning to crow*** (page 7)
   Male chickens usually make a loud noise, early in the morning. These are the cockerels crowing.
2. ***sound of the waves on the beach*** (page 7)
   the noise made by the sea hitting the land.
3. ***corncakes*** (page 9)
   a kind of bread.
4. ***neighbours*** (page 10)
   people who live in houses near to one another.
5. ***wound*** (page 12)
   in this case, the hole made by the sharp sting of a scorpion.
6. ***beggars*** (page 14)
   poor people who ask for money and for food.
7. ***race*** (page 15)
   The doctor and Kino belong to different races. The doctor is a European and comes from Spain; Kino is a South American Indian. People from different races often have different coloured skins and their heads and faces are sometimes different in shape.
8. ***ashamed*** (page 17)
   feeling unhappy because you or someone else has done something wrong. Also, feeling unhappy because you cannot help someone in trouble.
9. ***plaster*** (page 18)
   a thick, wet mixture which is smoothed onto wood or stone. When it dries, it becomes hard.
10. ***seaweed*** (page 18)
    plants which grow under water.
11. ***oyster beds*** (page 19)
    places under the sea where oysters live.
12. ***repairs*** (page 24)
    the things you do to make something whole again.
13. ***plans*** (page 25)
    decisions about what you hope to do in the future.
14. ***insects*** (page 29)
    small creatures like flies or moths. Some insects, like cicadas for example, make a loud noise.

15 **hate** (page 30)
   a strong feeling of dislike.
16 **destroy** (page 39)
   to do great harm to someone or something.
17 **greedy** (page 40)
   a greedy man wants everything for himself.
18 **cheat** (page 42)
   to deceive or trick a person by not giving him the right amount of money.
19 **fair price** (page 42)
   a price which is good for the person who is selling and the person who is buying.
20 **capital** (page 42)
   the main city of a country.
21 **cruel** (page 64)
   without feelings of love or pity for another person.
22 **tracks** (page 64)
   marks made on the ground by a person or a cart or an animal.
23 **sweat** (page 80)
   sweat is moisture which appears on your skin when you are very hot or afraid.
24 **puppies** (page 81)
   young dogs.

Exercises

Background information and characters

Choose the correct information to complete the sentences.

1 Kino hoped that a large pearl would bring (happiness) / fear to his family.

2 Kino had a moustache / beard.

3 Kino made money by finding fish / pearls in the sea.

4 Kino felt calm / afraid when he thought about someone stealing the pearl.

5 Both Kino and Juana / Neither Kino nor Juana had black hair.

6 Kino and Juana lived in the centre of town / near the sea.

7 Kino and Juana's house was made of stone / wood.

8 Juana was a weak / strong woman.

9 Kino and the doctor came from different races / lived in different towns.

10 The doctor was a mean / generous man.

11 The servant felt ashamed / afraid when the doctor wouldn't see Kino and his family.

12 The beggars slept in front of the doctor's gate / church.

Words from the story

Match the words in the box with the definitions.

| shadow | tracks | basket | canoe | race | leather | ~~scorpion~~ | cruel |
| pool | waves | plaster | cave | tracker | shawl | gate | beggar |

1 An animal like a large insect with a long body and a tail which has a dangerous sting.	*scorpion*
2 A strong material made from animal skin that is used for making clothes, shoes and bags.	

3 Marks that a person, animal or vehicle leaves on the ground.	
4 A bag made from thin pieces of wood, plastic or metal. Can be used to carry shopping.	
5 A door outside, often between a street and a garden.	
6 A dark area caused by someone or something stopping the light.	
7 Someone who follows clues to find another person.	
8 A small, narrow boat which is pointed at both ends.	
9 Causing pain to people or animals, without feelings of pity or love.	
10 A large piece of material that women wear on their shoulders or head, or use to cover a baby.	
11 A very poor person who lives by asking people for money or food.	
12 A large hole in the side of a hill or mountain, or under the ground.	
13 Lines of water that rise up on the surface of a sea, lake or river.	
14 A thick substance you put on walls to make them smooth and hard.	
15 A small area of water.	
16 A group of people with the same physical characteristics and customs.	

Sounds

Put the words from the box on page 91 into the correct sound categories.

/ɑː/	/uː/	/ɔː/
plant	food	floor

/e/	/eɪ/	/æ/
ins<u>e</u>ct	n<u>ei</u>ghbours	man

Put the words in the gaps

Use the words in the box to complete the sentences.

> cheat   ashamed   destroy   rifle   puppies   mat   sweat
> greedy   wound   ~~poison~~   seaweed   prayers   servant

1 When an insect stung Coyotito, the ......*poison*...... made him very ill.

2 Kino and Juana went to sleep on a .... on the floor.

3 The sting broke the baby's skin and made a ....

4 The doctor employed a .... to do jobs such as cooking and cleaning.

5 Kino dreamt of having a long gun called a ....

6 When her baby became ill, Juana said .... to her god.

7 Juana was afraid that the pearl would .... her family.

8 Juana used a plant that grows in the sea called .... to make Coyotito better.

9 The buyers wanted to .... Kino by giving him a small amount of money.

10 After Kino hit his wife he knew it was wrong and felt ....

11 When Kino climbed down the mountain he became very hot and this made him ....

12 The trackers heard noises which they thought were baby dogs called ....

13 The people didn't want Kino to be .... and keep all the money for himself.

Irregular past verbs

a **Write the past simple form of the verbs.**

Infinitive	Past simple	Infinitive	Past simple
beat		shake	
blow		shine	
bring		sing	
burn		sleep	
dream		smell	
hide		spit	
hold		sting	
kneel		teach	
lie		throw	

Which three verbs have two past simple forms?
Which past simple form is the same as the infinitive?

b **Write the correct form of the verbs from a in the gaps.**

1 When he needed to rest Kino ..... *lay* ..... on his mat.

2 At night Kino and Juana .... on the mat.

3 Kino .... the pearl in the ground to keep it safe.

4 When Kino left the village, his hand started to .... with emotion.

5 The weather was beautiful and the sun .... every day.

6 Kino .... of owning a rifle.

7 An insect .... Coyotito.

8 Juana liked to .... songs.

9 When Juana saw the pearl on the path she .... down to pick it up.

10 Juana wanted to .... the pearl back into the water.

11 Every morning Juana made corncakes and Kino .... the cooking.

12 Kino and Juana's house was made from wood so it .... easily.

13 Juana .... on the fire so that it would burn.

Multiple choice

Tick the best answer.

1 What happened to Coyotito?
 a A spider stung him.
 b A scorpion stung him. ✓
 c A bee stung him.

2 Where did Kino and Juana take the baby?
 a To the priest.
 b To a neighbour.
 c To a doctor.

3 Why did the doctor refuse to see the baby?
 a Because Kino and Juana didn't have any money.
 b Because he was too busy.
 c Because he didn't know how to treat the baby.

4 Why was Kino's canoe valuable?
   a It was expensive.
   b It was new.
   c It was used to find food.

5 What did Kino find at the bottom of the sea?
   a A basket.
   b A very big pearl.
   c Some seaweed.

6 What happened to Coyotito while Kino was opening the oyster?
   a His condition got worse.
   b He began to get better.
   c He started to cry.

7 Who visited Kino's house after he had found the pearl?
   a The neighbours.
   b The priest and the doctor.
   c The priest, the doctor and the neighbours.

8 How many times did the doctor visit Kino?
   a Once.
   b Twice.
   c Three times.

9 How did Kino feel that evening?
   a Excited about the future.
   b Worried about Coyotito.
   c Afraid someone would steal the pearl.

10 What did the buyers offer Kino for the pearl?
   a Less money than its value.
   b A good price.
   c More money than its value.

11 Why did Juana take the pearl?
   a To throw it back in the sea.
   b To hide it.
   c To steal it for herself.

12 What happened to the stranger who attacked Kino?
   a He stole the pearl.
   b Kino killed him.
   c Kino wounded him.

13 Who found the pearl after the attack?
   a Kino.
   b An attacker.
   c Juana.

14 Why did Kino decide to run away?
   a He had killed a man.
   b His house had burnt down.
   c His canoe was destroyed.

15 Who followed the family?
   a Trackers.
   b The neighbours.
   c The doctor.

16 Where did Juana hide with Coyotito when Kino went to confront the men?
   a In the trees.
   b In a cave.
   c In a valley.

17 What happened to Coyotito?
   a He got better.
   b He was killed.
   c He fell down the mountain.

Adjective order

Look at the example and then put the words in the correct order.

> The usual order of adjectives is:
> opinion, size, age, shape, colour, origin, material + noun
> **Example:** Juana had *an old blue skirt*.

1 a / man / young / strong

2 a / silk / dressing gown / red

3 pearls / ugly / grey

4 a / shiny / beautiful / pearl

5 a / black / small / insect

6 a(n) / old / shawl / dirty

7 a(n) / white / canoe / ancient

8 a / mountain / rocky / high

9 a / house / small / stone

10 a / square / basket / metal

Grammar focus: third conditional

Change the sentences to make them similar to the examples.

> **Example 1:** The scorpion stung Coyotito and he became ill.
> *If the scorpion hadn't stung Coyotito, he wouldn't have become ill.*
>
> **Example 2:** Kino didn't have any money and so the doctor didn't treat his son.
> *If Kino had had some money, the doctor would have treated his son.*

1 Kino and Juana were poor so they didn't get married in church.

2 The doctor refused to treat his son and Kino got angry.

3 Kino went to dive for pearls and found the largest pearl in the world.

4 Kino had a valuable pearl so the doctor gave Coyotito medicine.

5 The buyers were greedy and didn't offer Kino a good price for the pearl.

6 The buyers didn't offer a good price so Kino decided to go to the city.

7 Juana didn't throw the pearl back into the sea and the family had more bad luck.

8 A man tried to steal the pearl and Kino killed him.

9 Because Kino found a valuable pearl, someone burnt his house down.

10 Kino killed a man and ran away with Juana and Coyotito.

11 They ran away and trackers followed them.

12 They needed water so they went down into a valley.

13 The trackers followed them and so they hid in a cave.

14 Coyotito cried and a tracker shot him.

Published by Macmillan Heinemann ELT
Between Towns Road, Oxford OX4 3PP
A division of Macmillan Publishers Limited
Companies and representatives throughout the world
Heinemann is the registered trademark of Pearson Education, used under licence.

ISBN 978–0–2300–3113–5
ISBN 978–0–2300–3112–8 (With CD pack)

The Pearl by John Steinbeck copyright © John Steinbeck
This retold version by for Macmillan Readers.

First published 1991
This edition published 2009
Text © Macmillan Publishers Limited 2009
Design and illustration © Macmillan Publishers Limited 2009

All rights reserved; no part of this publication may be
reproduced, stored in a retrieval system, transmitted in any
form, or by any means, electronic, mechanical, photocopying,
recording, or otherwise, without the prior written permission of
the publishers.

Illustrated by Phyllis Mahon
Cover photograph by Corbis / Condé Nast Archive

Printed and bound in Thailand

2012 2011 2010
8 7 6 5 4

With CD pack
2012 2011 2010
7 6 5 4 3